# Hidden Picture Mazes

## Conceptis Puzzles

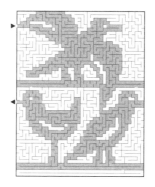

Sterling Publishing Co., Inc.

New York

To find out more about Conceptis Puzzles,
visit www.conceptispuzzles.com

10  9  8  7  6  5  4  3  2

Published by Sterling Publishing Co., Inc.
387 Park Avenue South, New York, NY 10016
©2005 by Conceptis Puzzles
Distributed in Canada by Sterling Publishing
$c/o$ Canadian Manda Group, 165 Dufferin Street
Toronto, Ontario, Canada M6K 3H6
Distributed in Great Britain and Europe by Chris Lloyd at Orca Book
Services, Stanley House, Fleets Lane, Poole BH15 3AJ, England
Distributed in Australia by Capricorn Link (Australia) Pty. Ltd.
P.O. Box 704, Windsor, NSW 2756, Australia

Sterling ISBN 1-4027-2491-8

For information about custom editions, special sales, premium and
corporate purchases, please contact Sterling Special Sales Department
at 800-805-5489 or specialsales@sterlingpub.com.

# Contents

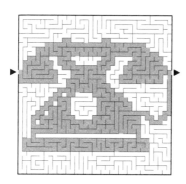

# Introduction

Solve a maze and create a picture! There are two types of picture maze puzzles in this book, basic and reversed. To start out, solve each of these fun puzzles just as you would a traditional maze: find the true path by starting at the maze's entrance and drawing a line to the maze's exit, avoiding false paths and dead ends.

But the fun is not over once you exit! What's next? In the basic kind of maze, you color in the path you traced with a dark, thick line of pen or marker to create a picture. In the other kind, which we call the reversed maze (labeled **R**), after you have traced the true path lightly in pencil, color in all the wrong paths with a thick pen or pencil to create your picture.

You might be surprised to learn that picture mazes of this kind were invented in Japan over 20 years ago. Today picture mazes have a dedicated following among children and adults all over the world. By reversing the tones of the maze paths, we are able to offer you more detailed pictures than are available with basic picture mazes alone, as well as recognizable portrait mazes. So grab your marker and pencil and get started!

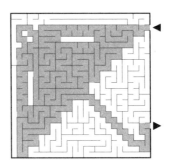

# Maze #1

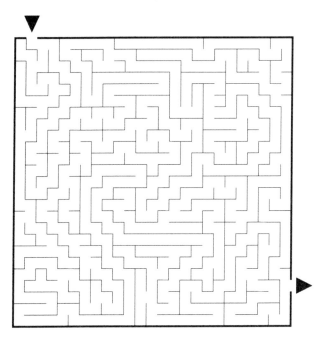

## Maze #2

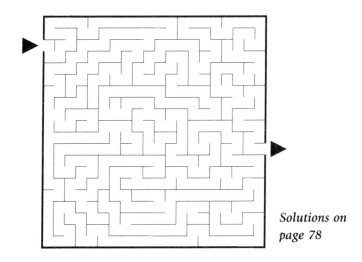

*Solutions on
page 78*

# Maze #3

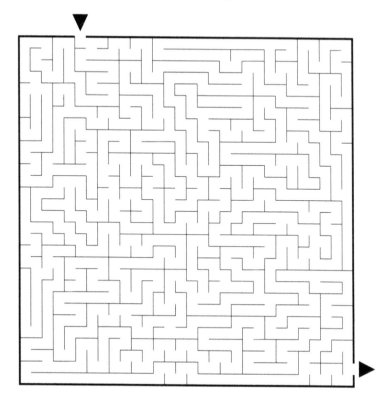

*Solution on page 78*

# Maze #4

*Solution on page 78*

*Solution on page 78*

*Solution on page 79*

# Maze #7

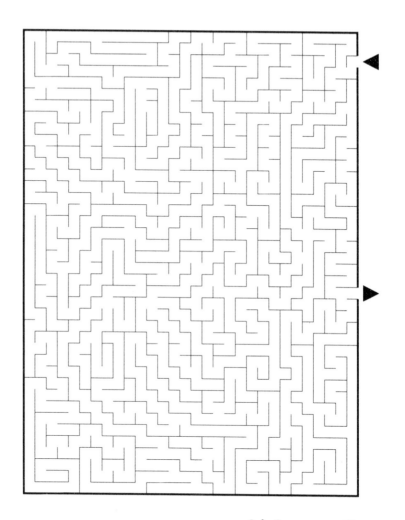

*Solution on page 79*

# Maze #8

*Solution on page 79*

*Solution on page 79*

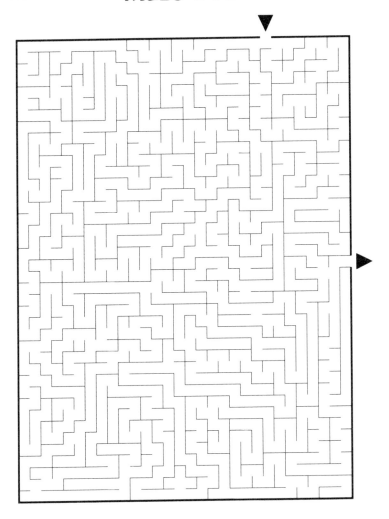

*Solution on page 80*

# Maze #11

*Solution on page 80*

*Solution on page 80*

*Solution on page 80*

*Solution on page 81*

*Solution on page 81*

*Solution on page 81*

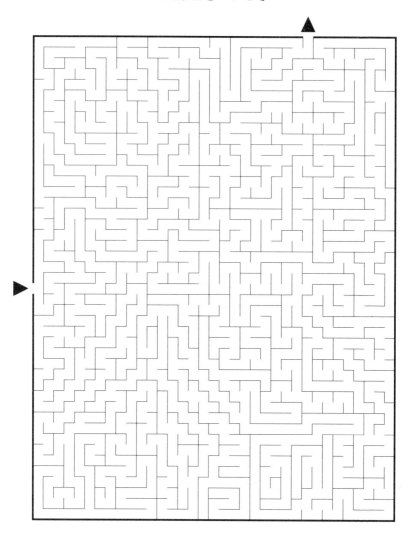

*Solution on page 81*

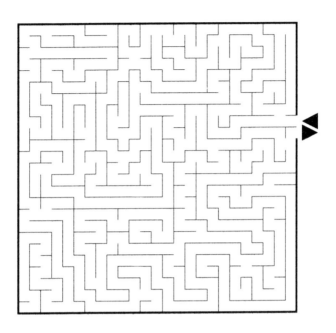

## Maze #19

*Solutions on page 82*

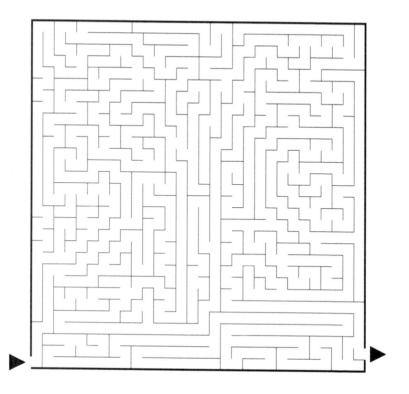

*Solution on page 82*

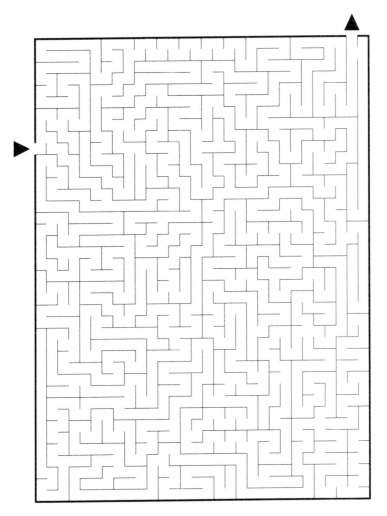

*Solution on page 82*

*Solution on page 82*

*Solution on page 83*

# Maze #24

*Solution on page 83*

*Solution on page 83*

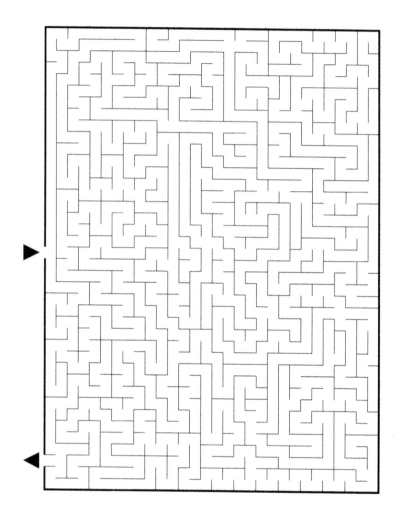

*Solution on page 83*

# Maze #27

*Solution on page 84*

*Solution on page 84*

*Solution on page 84*

# Maze #30

*Solution on page 84*

*Solution on page 85*

*Solution on page 85*

# Maze #33

*Solution on page 85*

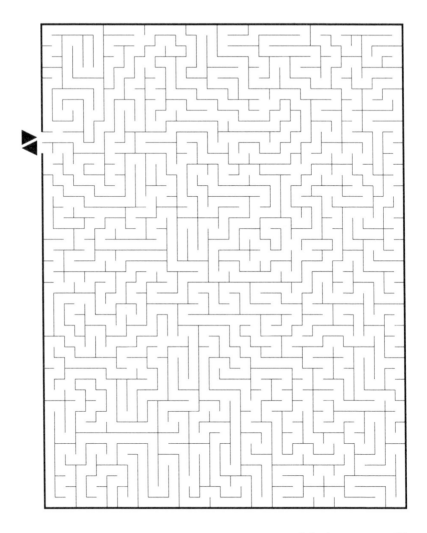

*Solution on page 85*

# Maze #35

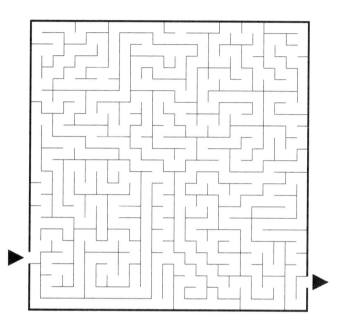

## Maze #36

*Solutions on page 86*

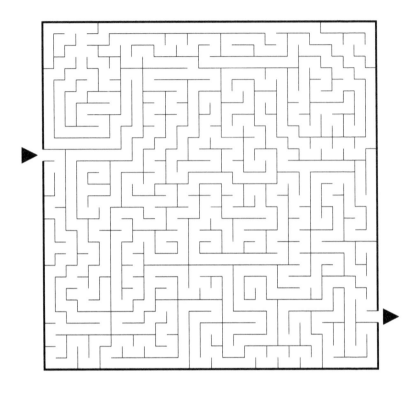

*Solution on page 86*

*Solution on page 86*

*Solution on page 86*

*Solution on page 87*

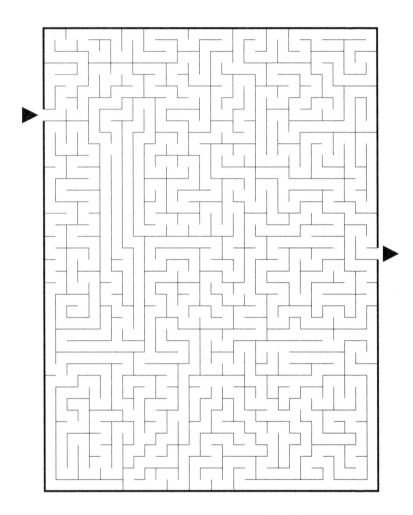

*Solution on page 87*

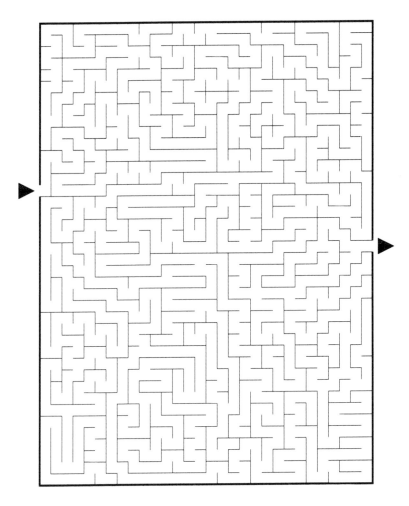

*Solution on page 87*

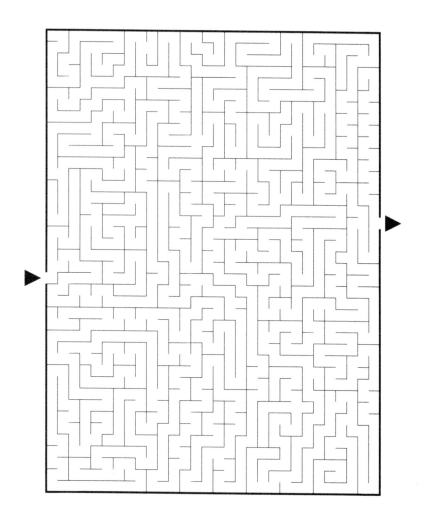

*Solution on page 87*

*Solution on page 88*

*Solution on page 88*

*Solution on page 88*

# Maze #47

*Solution on page 88*

*Solution on page 89*

*Solution on page 89*

# Maze #50

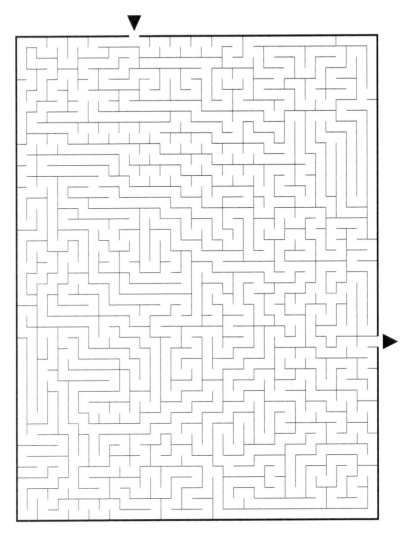

*Solution on page 89*

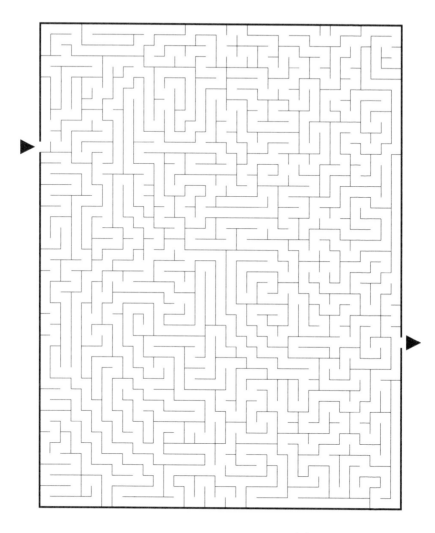

*Solution on page 89*

# Maze #52

*Solution on page 90*

*Solution on page 90*

# Maze #54

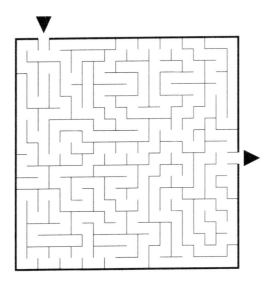

# Maze #55

*Solutions on page 90*

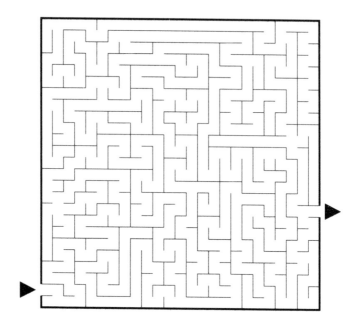

*Solution on page 90*

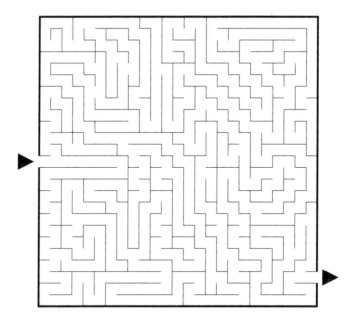

*Solution on page 91*

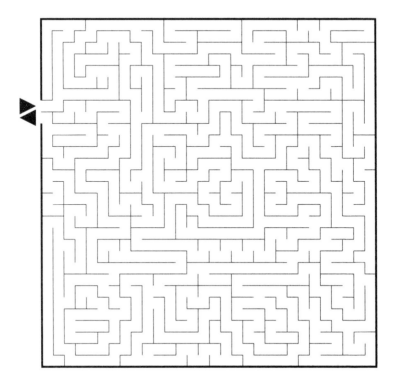

*Solution on page 91*

# Maze #59

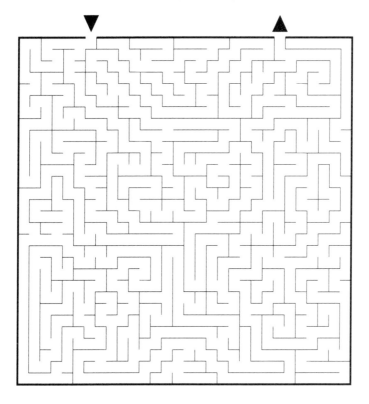

*Solution on page 91*

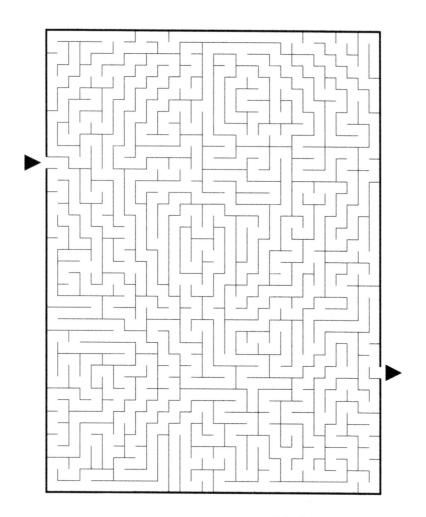

*Solution on page 91*

# Maze #61

*Solution on page 91*

# Maze #62

*Solution on page 92*

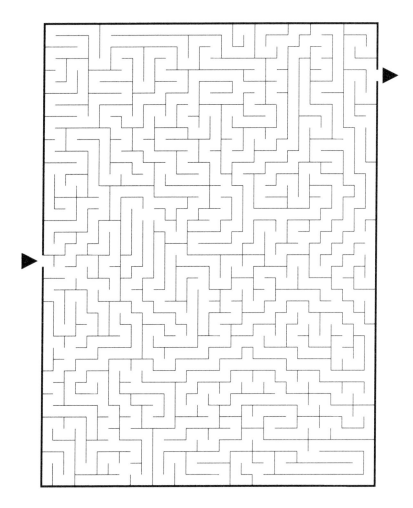

*Solution on page 92*

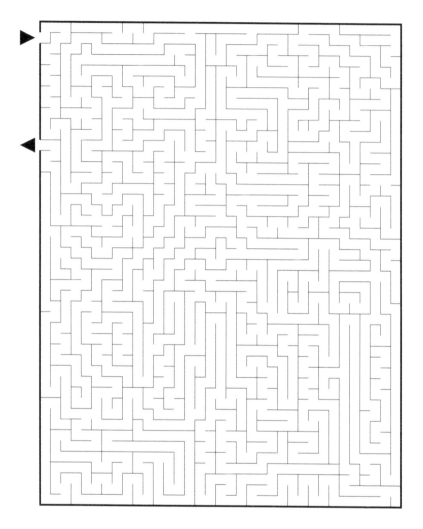

*Solution on page 92*

*Solution on page 92*

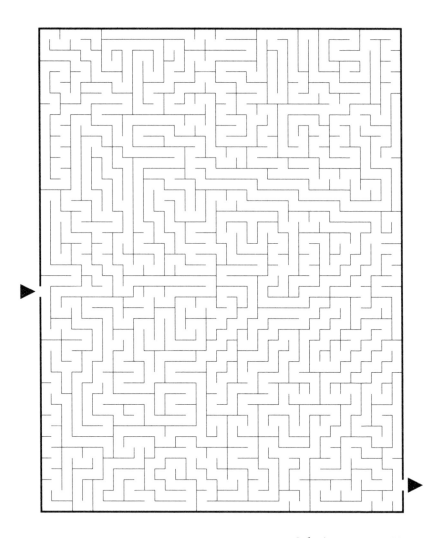

*Solution on page 93*

# Maze #67

*Solution on page 93*

*Solution on page 93*

*Solution on page 94*

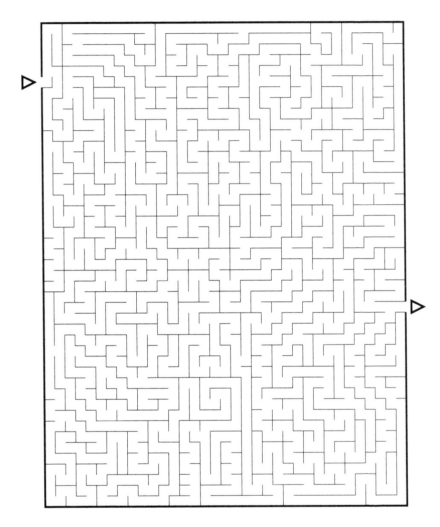

*Solution on page 94*

**R** This is a reversed maze. After you have traced the true path (solution) lightly in pencil, color in all the wrong paths with a thick pen or pencil to create your picture.

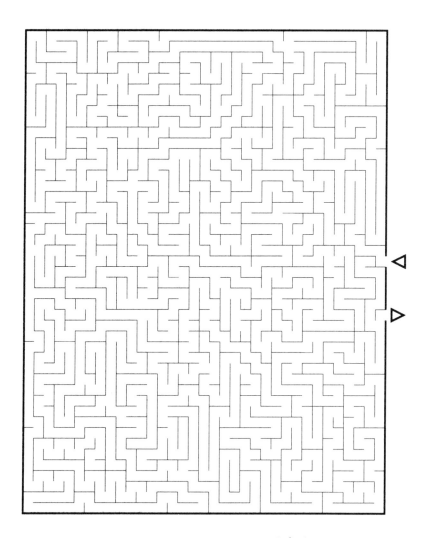

*Solution on page 94*

**R** This is a reversed maze. After you have traced the true path (solution) lightly in pencil, color in all the wrong paths with a thick pen or pencil to create your picture.

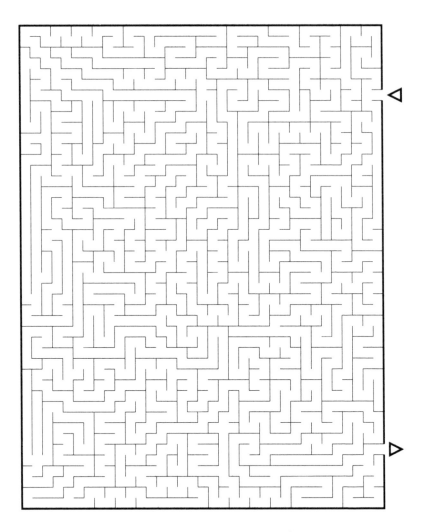

*Solution on page 95*

This is a reversed maze. After you have traced the true path (solution) lightly in pencil, color in all the wrong paths with a thick pen or pencil to create your picture.

*Solution on page 95*

**R** This is a reversed maze. After you have traced the true path (solution) lightly in pencil, color in all the wrong paths with a thick pen or pencil to create your picture.

*Solution on page 95*

**R** This is a reversed maze. After you have traced the true path (solution) lightly in pencil, color in all the wrong paths with a thick pen or pencil to create your picture.

# Maze #75

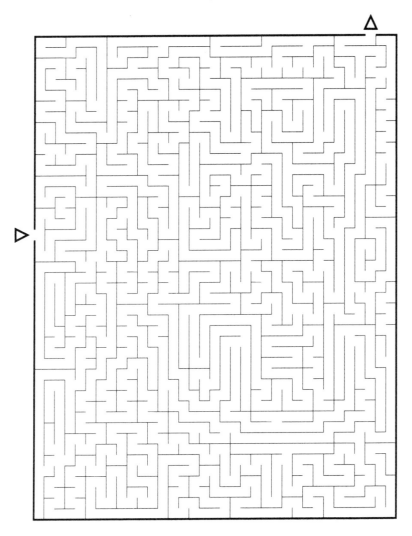

*Solution on page 96*

**R** This is a reversed maze. After you have traced the true path (solution) lightly in pencil, color in all the wrong paths with a thick pen or pencil to create your picture.

# Maze #76

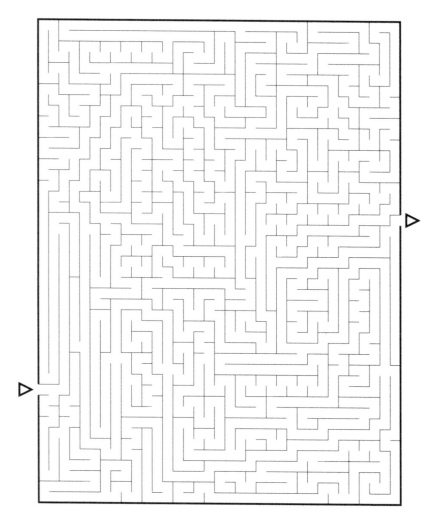

*Solution on page 96*

**R** This is a reversed maze. After you have traced the true path (solution) lightly in pencil, color in all the wrong paths with a thick pen or pencil to create your picture.

*Solution on page 96*

**R** This is a reversed maze. After you have traced the true path (solution) lightly in pencil, color in all the wrong paths with a thick pen or pencil to create your picture.

# Solutions

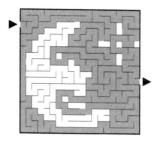

*Maze on page 5*

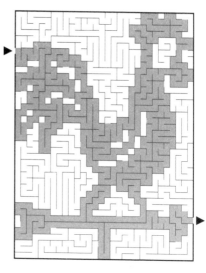

*Maze on page 7*

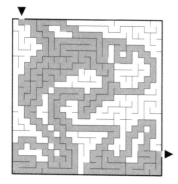

*Maze on page 5*

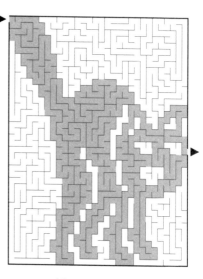

*Maze on page 8*

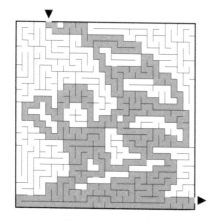

*Maze on page 6*

# Solutions

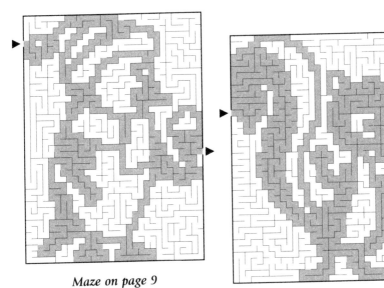

Maze on page 9

Maze on page 11

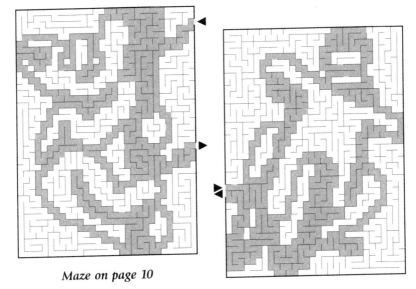

Maze on page 10

Maze on page 12

# Solutions

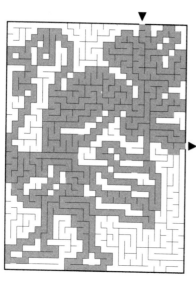

Maze on page 13

Maze on page 15

Maze on page 14

Maze on page 16

# Solutions

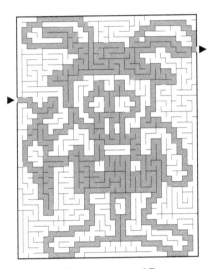

*Maze on page 17*

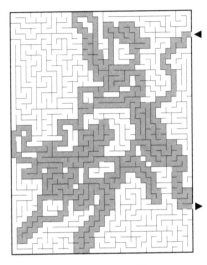

*Maze on page 19*

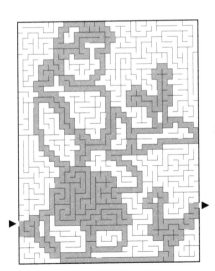

*Maze on page 18*

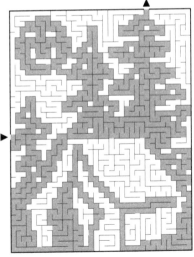

*Maze on page 20*

# Solutions

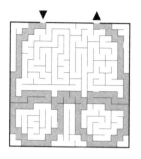

*Maze on page 21*

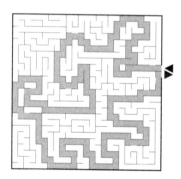

*Maze on page 21*

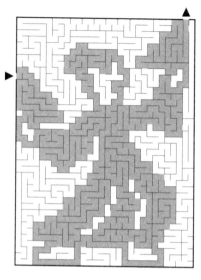

*Maze on page 23*

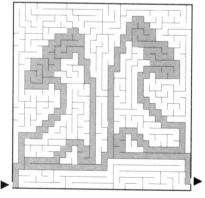

*Maze on page 22*

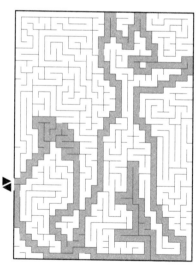

*Maze on page 24*

# Solutions

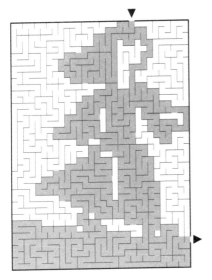

*Maze on page 25*

*Maze on page 27*

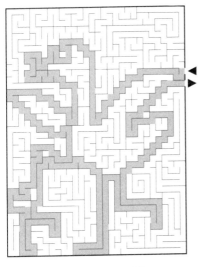

*Maze on page 26*

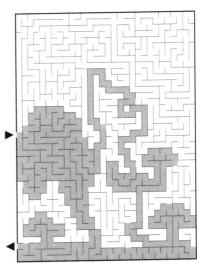

*Maze on page 28*

# Solutions

*Maze on page 29*

*Maze on page 31*

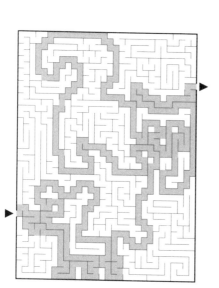

*Maze on page 30*

*Maze on page 32*

# Solutions

Maze on page 33

Maze on page 35

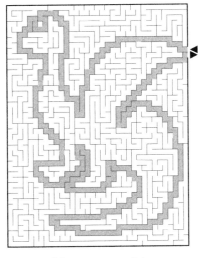

Maze on page 34

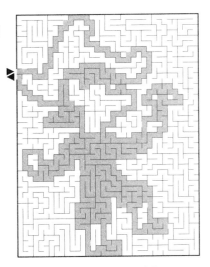

Maze on page 36

# Solutions

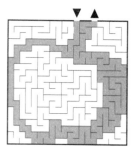

*Maze on page 37*

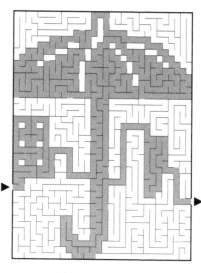

*Maze on page 39*

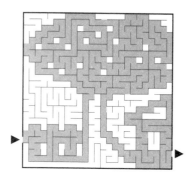

*Maze on page 37*

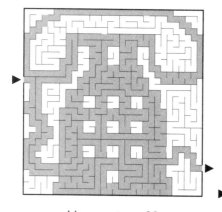

*Maze on page 38*

*Maze on page 40*

# Solutions

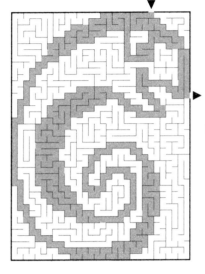

*Maze on page 41*

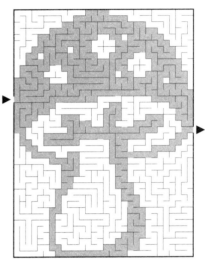

*Maze on page 43*

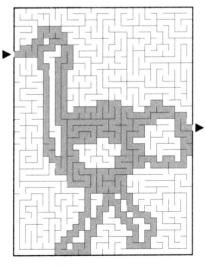

*Maze on page 42*

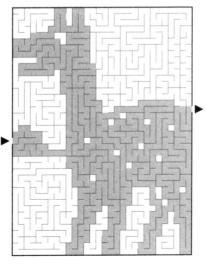

*Maze on page 44*

# Solutions

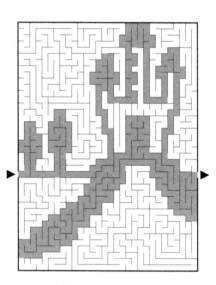

*Maze on page 47*

*Maze on page 45*

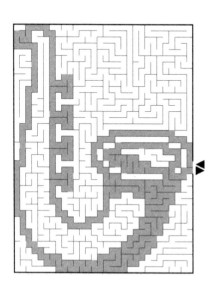

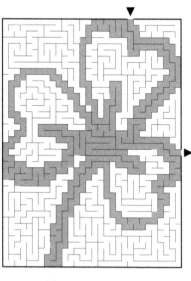

*Maze on page 46*

*Maze on page 48*

# Solutions

*Maze on page 49*

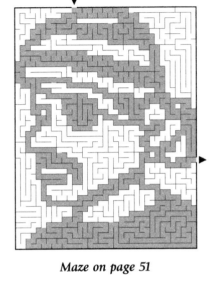

*Maze on page 51*

*Maze on page 50*

*Maze on page 52*

# Solutions

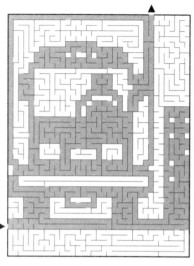

*Maze on page 53*

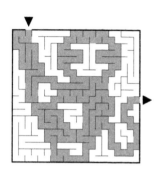

*Maze on page 55*

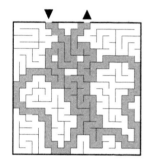

*Maze on page 55*

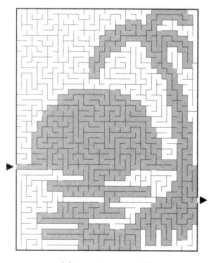

*Maze on page 54*

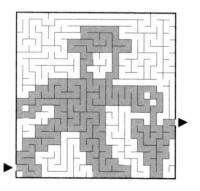

*Maze on page 56*

# Solutions

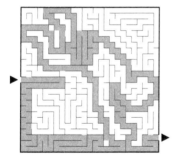

*Maze on page 57*

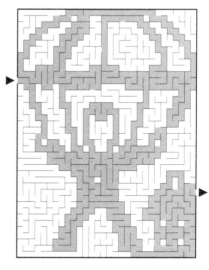

*Maze on page 60*

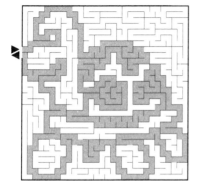

*Maze on page 58*

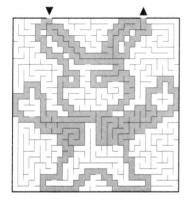

*Maze on page 59*

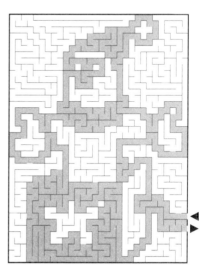

*Maze on page 61*

# Solutions

Maze on page 62

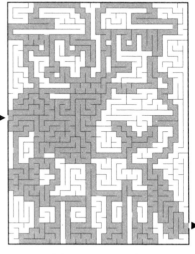

Maze on page 64

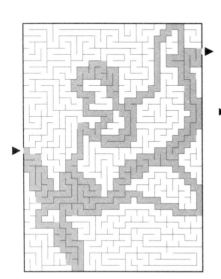

Maze on page 63

Maze on page 65

# Solutions

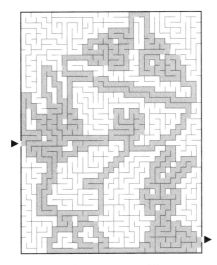

*Maze on page 66*

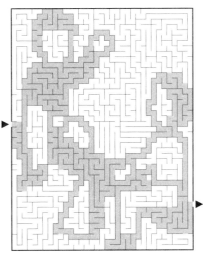

*Maze on page 68*

*Maze on page 67*

# Solutions

*Maze on page 69*

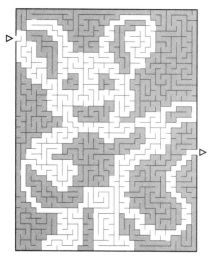

*Maze on page 71*

*Maze on page 70*

# Solutions

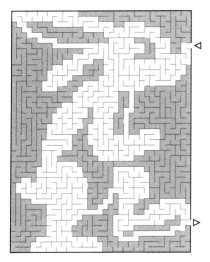

*Maze on page 72*

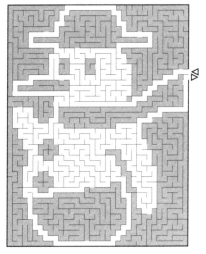

*Maze on page 74*

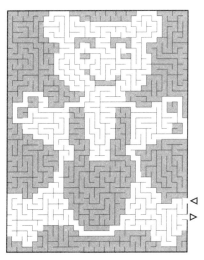

*Maze on page 73*

# Solutions

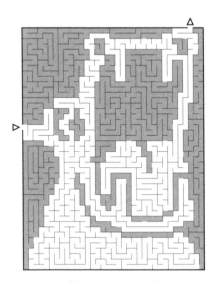

Maze on page 75

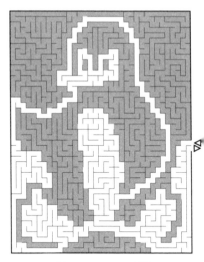

Maze on page 77

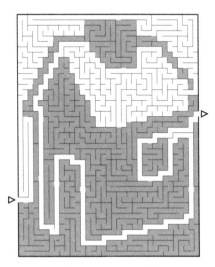

Maze on page 76